Discarded

the extreme sports collection

skydiving!

take the leap

by Jeremy Roberts

rosen publishing group's

rosen central

new york

For Bobby, our biggest leap yet.

Published in 1999 by The Rosen Publishing Group, Inc.
29 East 21st Street, New York, NY 10010

Copyright © 1999 by The Rosen Publishing Group, Inc.

First Edition 1999

Library of Congress Cataloging-in-Publication Data

Roberts, Jeremy
     Skydiving! take the leap / Jeremy Roberts.
          p. cm.—(The extreme sports collection)
     Includes bibliographical references (p. 61) and index.
     Summary: Discusses the history of skydiving, the different kinds and maneuvers, the equipment, and the nature of skydiving as an extreme sport.
     ISBN 0-8239-3015-7 (lib. bdg.)
     1. Skydiving Juvenile literature. [1. Skydiving.] I. Title. II. Series.
GV770.R597 1999
99-13205
CIP

Manufactured in the United States of America

contents

Extremely Interesting

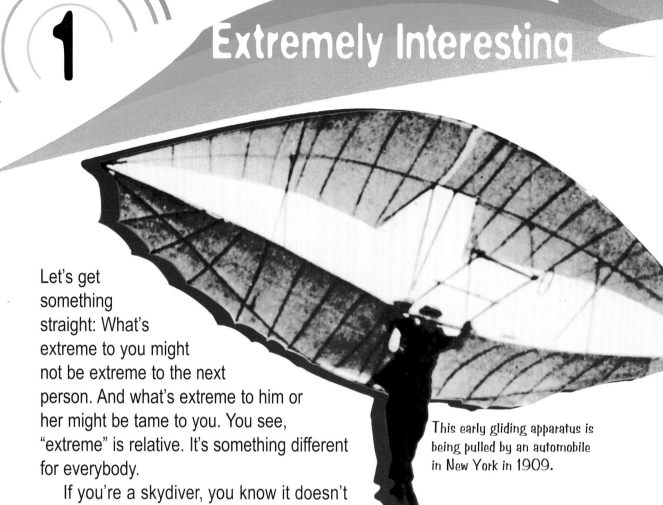

This early gliding apparatus is being pulled by an automobile in New York in 1909.

Let's get something straight: What's extreme to you might not be extreme to the next person. And what's extreme to him or her might be tame to you. You see, "extreme" is relative. It's something different for everybody.

If you're a skydiver, you know it doesn't get more extreme than this: You. The sky. Gravity. Put all three together at anywhere from 2,000 to over 10,000 feet, and you have skydiving. It's a sport that has been around for 200 years—but its newest form, skysurfing, is less than 10 years old.

Skydiving may be the ultimate individualistic sport. Skydivers jump from terrifyingly high heights, or altitudes. Once they leave the airplane, they are free to do nearly anything they want—but only for about a minute or so. Although they may look like they're floating in midair, skydivers are actually falling very quickly toward the ground.

This midair flying is called freefall. For many skydivers, it's the most exciting part of the trip. During freefall a skydiver can do special tricks and moves. Some skydivers

Extreme Fact

Most skysurfers jump out of the airplane at around 14,000 feet above the earth.

make formations or shapes in the air by linking their bodies with others. Skysurfers climb onto skyboards, sort of like air skateboards, and strut their stuff. For humans, freefall is like flying without wings.

Skydivers join together in a planned pattern.

Freefall has its dangers. At terminal velocity, which is as fast as a skydiver can fall, he or she is hurtling downward at over 100 miles per hour. No matter what tricks the skydiver performs, he or she has to be finished before the earth gets too close. There is a minimum distance from the ground that skydivers can safely deploy their parachutes. If the ripcord isn't pulled before the diver reaches this distance, there may not be enough time for the parachute to fill with air and slow the skydiver down. And if the skydiver's fall isn't slowed down . . . well, that's bad news.

Opening the parachute (or "chute") slows skydivers down, but it doesn't end the fun. Modern parachutes, also called canopies, are designed to be flown by the skydiver. These are like personal airplanes. A really good sky-diver can fly in circles through the air and land on a quarter. It's beyond awesome—it's extreme.

Terminal velocity is the fastest speed at which a skydiver can fall. Gravity pulls at everything equally, but drag, or wind resistance, makes terminal velocity different for each object. Before pulling the rip-cord, skydivers usually reach a terminal velocity of 120 to 135 miles per hour.

Today there are the X Games, a sort of miniature Olympics for extreme sports. Athletes from around the world gather for this event to show just how extreme they can be. They climb ice walls, race down slippery, snow-covered ski slopes on mountain bikes, and surf through the sky. They compete to see who can grab the biggest air, who can hit the highest speeds, and who can perform the most difficult stunts. The winners are given gold medals and the title of "Most Extreme Athlete on the Planet." At least, that is, until the next X Games, when new athletes redefine what it means to be extreme.

Another version of extreme sports takes place behind the scenes, away from the glory that comes with television coverage and cheering crowds. These athletes prefer to play alone, with only nature and the elements for company. They're the mountain climbers, the backcountry bikers and snowboarders, the explorers. They'll never get a gold medal for what they do, and they probably wouldn't want one anyway. They're doing it because they love it, not because it attracts a crowd.

Most people agree that for a sport to be extreme, it has to be difficult—at least for the beginner. It requires specialized skills and techniques. It also requires an adventurous attitude—the kind of attitude that says there are no limits. Whether this means skydiving solo, jumping while tied to an instructor, or just getting on the plane for the first time, it all depends on you: what you're willing or not willing to try.

Extreme sports can be dangerous, but being extreme doesn't mean being foolish or taking unnecessary risks. No skydiver wants to

Extreme Fact

Most skydivers deploy their parachutes at around 2,000 to 2,500 feet above the ground.

risk an injury that might mean never diving again. You can be extreme and still follow safety rules.

Skydiving, like ice climbing and snowboarding, is popular with people who want to live on the edge. Like other extreme sports, skydivers have their own way of talking, moving, and dressing. Whether they're skysurfing—the ultimate extreme sport—or performing a high-altitude jump in the middle of the night, skydivers live for the rush.

Skydivers also have inspired others who don't take part in the sport. Television commercials for products that have a cool or cutting edge image often feature skysurfers. Jumping out of an airplane tells the world, "I've got attitude." And altitude.

Extreme terms are now part of our everyday language. Technology that has made extreme sports possible and popular is all around us. If you wear a fleece pullover or put on a lightweight but protective helmet, you're benefiting from extreme sports and their culture.

Of course, skydivers are a little different. After all, they hang out at 5,000 feet.

These extreme athletes are "hanging out" during the X Games.

2 Way Back When

Parachutes, the most important piece of sky-diving equipment, were being used even before airplanes were invented. There are many stories of people parachute jumping from high buildings and towers during the Middle Ages in Europe and China. Most of these stories are hard to prove. But we know for sure that Andre Jacques Garnerin was jumping from hot-air balloons over Paris in the early 1800s.

For nearly 100 years after that, various inventors improved the parachute. They made it safer and easier to use. During that time, parachutes were used as a way to get out of a balloon when something went wrong. They were also used to thrill crowds who liked to see people fall from the sky—and to thrill the parachutists themselves. We still use the parachute for the same reasons today.

In the early 1900s, during World War I, parachutes were used for emergencies involving balloons and airplanes. Those jumps were made

This illustration from 1783 shows a hot-air balloon taking off in France.

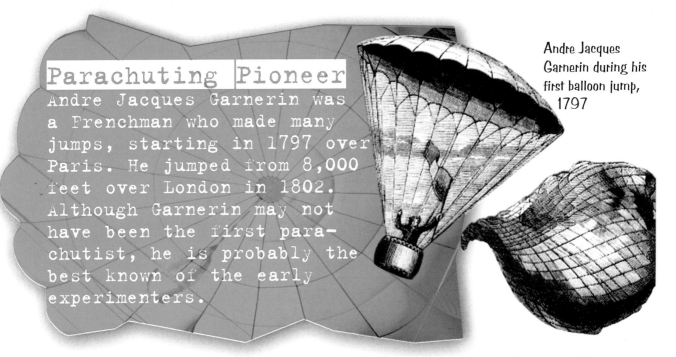

Parachuting Pioneer

Andre Jacques Garnerin was a Frenchman who made many jumps, starting in 1797 over Paris. He jumped from 8,000 feet over London in 1802. Although Garnerin may not have been the first parachutist, he is probably the best known of the early experimenters.

Andre Jacques Garnerin during his first balloon jump, 1797

with static lines. Static lines were attached to the balloons or airplanes and to the skydivers' parachutes. The lines detached after automatically deploying the chute at a specific distance from the airplane. "Deploy" means "to open" and is a word that skydivers use when they talk about opening their parachutes during a jump.

After World War I, freefall jumping became more popular. In freefall, the parachute doesn't deploy until the skydiver pulls a ripcord. It's called freefall jumping because the emphasis is on the longer freefall period of the jump—before the parachute deploys. More time in freefall means more time for tricks.

At first, sport skydivers, or people who skydived for fun, concentrated on accuracy. They wanted to steer toward an exact spot on the ground. That was very difficult with their parachutes. The chutes were designed in a round shape and were not easy to control. During the first parachute competition at the 1930

airborne troops

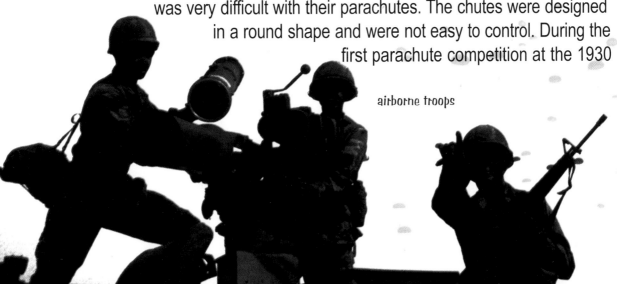

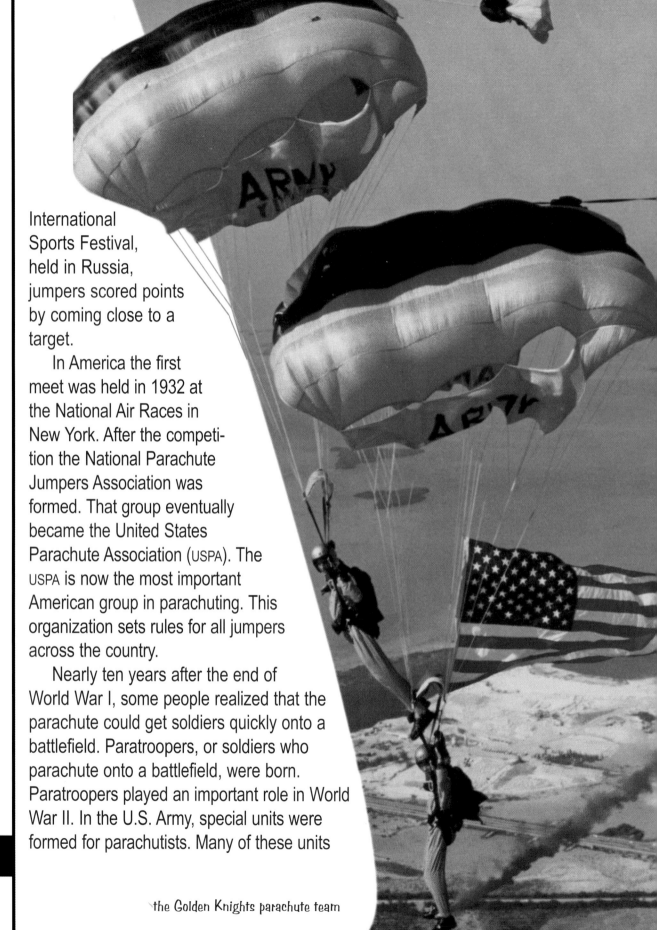

International
Sports Festival,
held in Russia,
jumpers scored points
by coming close to a
target.

In America the first
meet was held in 1932 at
the National Air Races in
New York. After the competition the National Parachute
Jumpers Association was
formed. That group eventually
became the United States
Parachute Association (USPA). The
USPA is now the most important
American group in parachuting. This
organization sets rules for all jumpers
across the country.

Nearly ten years after the end of
World War I, some people realized that the
parachute could get soldiers quickly onto a
battlefield. Paratroopers, or soldiers who
parachute onto a battlefield, were born.
Paratroopers played an important role in World
War II. In the U.S. Army, special units were
formed for parachutists. Many of these units

the Golden Knights parachute team

were termed "airborne" or "paratrooper."

After Word War II ended, the military tried to improve their equipment and style. Paratroopers wanted to be able to control where and how they came down. They took regular army parachutes and made radical changes to them. Many of their ideas helped sport skydivers. Soldiers were also among the best competitors. The U.S. Army's Golden Knights still strut their stuff in competitions and demonstrations throughout the world.

a freefall jump in New York during the 1960s

A lot of people started parachuting for fun in the 1950s and 1960s, and more competitions were held. There were usually two different types of contests. One was judged on accuracy. The closer a parachutist came to a target on the ground, the better his or her score. As in a track-and-field meet, there were a lot of different categories to keep things interesting. Skydivers could compete against others with about the same level of skill.

The U.S. National Forest Service established a team of skydivers to fight forest fires in 1934. They are called the Smoke Eaters.

11

Firefighters tumble from a command plane over the scene of a forest fire.

A second kind of parachuting competition also became popular. This was called freefall relative work. It all started when one skydiver passed a baton to another skydiver before pulling his ripcord. Soon other skydivers tried flying together after jumping from the airplane. They would form designs in the sky. Large numbers of jumpers began trying to form circles and stars in midair. The skydivers had to be quick and skilled because they had only a few minutes in the air before they got too close to the ground.

According to sports historians, the first eight-person star was formed in the 1960s in California. Soon there were ten-person competitions, which led to larger and larger numbers. A thirty-two-person star was formed in 1975. Less than ten years later, a seventy-two-person formation filled the skies over a competition. These days most people use the words "formation flying" instead of "relative work" to describe this type of parachuting, but they mean the same thing.

A record-breaking formation of 297 skydivers during a join-up operation. Achieving the correct position in a huge group is a major task.

As the design of parachutes became better and more maneuverable, another kind of relative work was invented: canopy formations. "Canopy" is another word for the part of a parachute that's usually made out of nylon. It's the square or round part of the equipment that fills with air and slows the skydiver's fall. When skydivers fly in canopy formations, they come together after pulling their ripcords instead of before. They maneuver their parachutes with great accuracy as they descend. This can be exciting to watch from the ground because the opened parachutes make the jumpers easy to see even from far away.

One of the newest forms of skydiving is skysurfing. A skysurfer "rides" a special skyboard through the air, performing tricks before it is time to pull the cord.

Skysurfing is a popular part of the X Games. It is also part of other competitions and air shows around the world. There are two members on each skysurfing team. One is the surfer, the other is the cameraperson. The surfer has to do a number of tricks before pulling the ripcord. These are judged on creativity and difficulty, just like an ice-skater in the Olympics.

Extreme Fact

Special Forces troops in the Gulf War parachuted into Iraq from special transport planes. Not only were they parachuting at night, but many opened their chutes at altitudes as high as 30,000 feet.

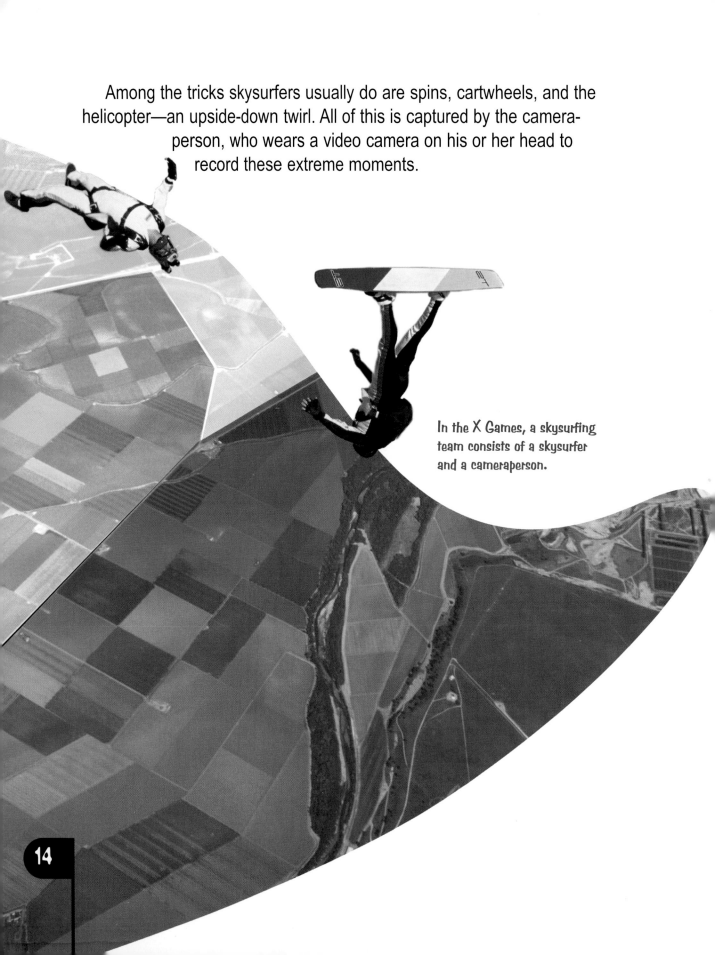

Among the tricks skysurfers usually do are spins, cartwheels, and the helicopter—an upside-down twirl. All of this is captured by the camera-person, who wears a video camera on his or her head to record these extreme moments.

In the X Games, a skysurfing team consists of a skysurfer and a cameraperson.

14

A skydiver needs some special gear before he or she can jump—much more than just a chute and a plane. Skydivers need equipment to help them stay safe, show off, and look cool.

The Rig

A skydiver's parachute and the equipment that makes it work is called a rig. The kind of rig a skydiver wears depends on what he or she wants to do in the air. But nearly all skydivers have at least two parachutes in their rig. These are the main parachute and a reserve parachute. The reserve is for emergencies and is hardly ever needed. But when it is, the skydiver is really happy that it's there!

Today nearly every parachute used in competition is a type called a ram-air canopy. It looks like a wedge made of several long cells, or sections. As the parachute descends, air fills these cells. The parachute becomes a miniature airplane wing. The skydiver can steer this type of chute very easily. Landings are very soft, at least compared to the early days. Some skydivers compare a good landing to walking off an escalator.

The ram-air parachute is also called a square. That's because its shape is different from the first parachutes, which were round. But you should know that even though it is called a square, the sides are shorter than the front and back.

Chutes can be designed in a variety of ways depending on what the skydiver wants to do. But almost all parachute rigs have the following parts:

The Pilot Chute

The pilot chute is a small parachute that opens the main parachute. It pops out when the ripcord is pulled. Because of its shape and size, it quickly fills with air. Once it is open, the pilot chute pulls out the main parachute, or main canopy. Without the pilot chute, it would take much longer for the main canopy to open. It also might not open properly.

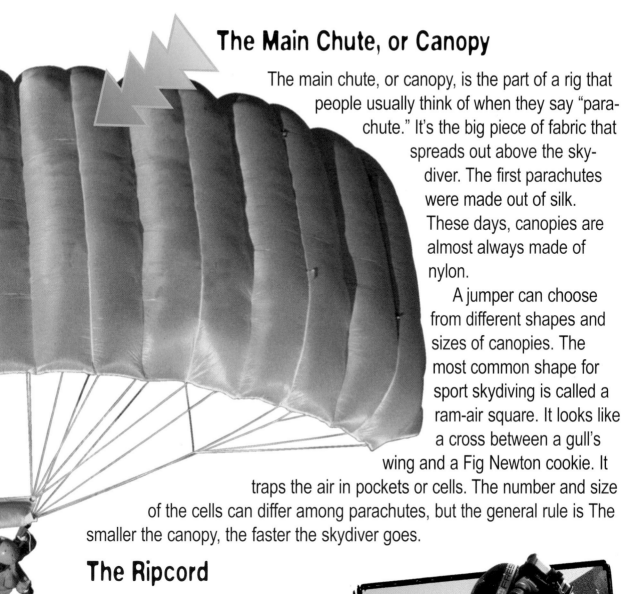

The Main Chute, or Canopy

The main chute, or canopy, is the part of a rig that people usually think of when they say "parachute." It's the big piece of fabric that spreads out above the skydiver. The first parachutes were made out of silk. These days, canopies are almost always made of nylon.

A jumper can choose from different shapes and sizes of canopies. The most common shape for sport skydiving is called a ram-air square. It looks like a cross between a gull's wing and a Fig Newton cookie. It traps the air in pockets or cells. The number and size of the cells can differ among parachutes, but the general rule is The smaller the canopy, the faster the skydiver goes.

The Ripcord

The ripcord is a handle that the skydiver pulls to release his or her pilot chute. It is easy to reach and is pulled with one hand. Pulling the ripcord gets everything going.

During some jumps, especially for a new skydiver, the ripcord isn't pulled by the jumper. The chute is deployed automatically by a line, or rope, attached to the airplane. This line is called a static line. The pilot chute can also be deployed by a special tool used for emergencies. And sometimes, experienced skydivers throw their pilot chutes out by hand.

The Harness

The harness includes the straps that attach the parachute to the skydiver's body and the ropes that are used to guide the parachute.

Other Equipment

There's more to parachuting than just the rig, however. Skydivers use a lot of other equipment.

Jumpsuit

Most skydivers wear a one-piece jumpsuit when they make a jump. Jumpsuits are usually very colorful; they help make a skydiver look cool when competing. But the designs aren't just for looks. Different designs are made for different styles of skydiving. Tight jumpsuits let sky-divers move through the air faster. Skysurfers, who must worry about wind resistance, wear these types of suits. Formation fliers, however, wear looser suits with special grips that make it easy for their partners to grab and hold on to them in midair.

Helmet

Not every skydiver wears a helmet. But helmets can prevent head injuries, just as they do for bikers or motorcyclists. Plus, helmets can make the skydiver look even cooler. Some helmets have face shields that make the divers look like astronauts.

Goggles

Jumping out of an airplane can bring tears to people's eyes. It's not because they're afraid: The rushing air starts a natural reaction, just like the tears you get in your eyes on a cold and windy day. Since tears can make vision blurry, which can be dangerous, skydivers wear goggles to protect their eyes from wind as well as from any stray objects—insects, birds, UFOs—that may fly into them during the jump.

Boots

Paratroopers wear heavy boots when they're parachuting. That's because they may have to march to battle after they land. Proper landing form and modern parachutes prevent most foot injuries, so sport skydivers generally wear lightweight shoes like sneakers or athletic shoes. But some wear sandals, and others even go barefoot! One thing skydivers never wear are shoes with open hooks for the laces. The hooks could catch on something at the worst possible moment.

Skyboard

Skysurfers use a skyboard that looks a lot like a snowboard or miniature surfboard. In fact, some of the first boards were really boogie boards, a special kind of small surfboard used by watersurfers for tricks.

Today's skyboards are designed for acrobatics in the air. The skyboard's size and weight depend on the skysurfer. Small boards can be easier to control. But a surfer can usually do better tricks with a bigger board.

Most boards are made of light metal and graphite. You probably use a form of graphite every day in your pencil. Tennis rackets and other items are often made of the same material. Every board has foot straps

Extreme Fact
Most skysurfers surf left foot forward, at least at first. Right foot forward is called "goofy-foot."

that look like oversized Velcro tabs. These are called bindings. Bindings can be released easily in an emergency to free the surfer's feet. Some skyboards even come with their own parachutes.

Cameras

Cameras have recently become an important part of parachuting. The only way to get a good picture of a skydiver is for another skydiver to take it. Almost every photo of a skydiver in action has been taken by another diver.

Most professional skydiving cameras are worn on the diver's head. Special versions of both video and still cameras fit on the helmet. Divers can also use movie cameras.

In some competitions the video is broadcast from the skydive cam. Fans on the ground have a bird's-eye view of the action as it happens thousands of feet over their heads.

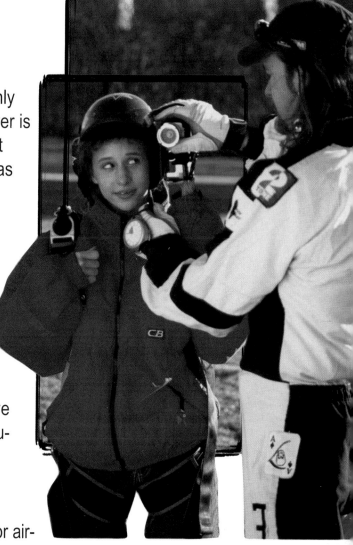

Planes

If it weren't for airplanes, most skydiving events would be "dirt jumps." That's a fancy way of saying "practice on the ground." Not very exciting.

Certain types of airplanes are better for skydiving than others. Slow, steady planes with high wings make it easier for skydivers to jump. Wide doorways are also a plus.

21

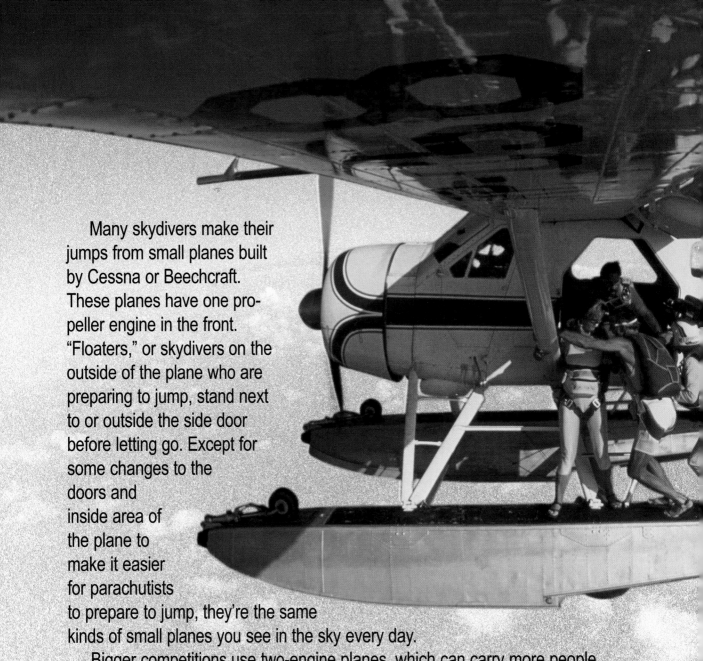

Many skydivers make their jumps from small planes built by Cessna or Beechcraft. These planes have one propeller engine in the front. "Floaters," or skydivers on the outside of the plane who are preparing to jump, stand next to or outside the side door before letting go. Except for some changes to the doors and inside area of the plane to make it easier for parachutists to prepare to jump, they're the same kinds of small planes you see in the sky every day.

Bigger competitions use two-engine planes, which can carry more people. Some open in the back, just like air force cargo planes. Popular two-engine planes include the Twin Otter and Skyvan.

So you've got your plane, your chute, your suit, and all your other gear. There are just a few more things that you need to know before you jump.

Three skydivers prepare to jump over the Pacific Ocean.

RP·C58

PARADISE

Skysurfing Sensations

Valery Rozov won the gold medal in the 1998 X Games at age 33. By that time he had already done more than 1,500 skysurfing jumps. Rozov had been skydiving for only about five years when he grabbed the gold. Camera jumper Clif Burch teamed up with Rozov, and the 1998 X Games brought him his second gold. Burch had finished first with Bob Greiner in 1996.

Staying Safe

Skydiving is considered a dangerous sport. But it can be very safe. Few people die in accidents even though their bodies zip through the air at over 100 miles per hour. In fact, some experts point out that a person is more likely to die in a car accident than skydiving.

How can something so dangerous also be safe? Skydivers take a lot of steps to make sure that they parachute safely. They have

The side door of this small plane has been altered so that skydivers can exit easily.

special equipment to help them if something goes wrong. They also must have a lot of training before they jump.

The Reserve Parachute

A skydiver's most important piece of emergency equipment is a backup, or reserve, parachute. A reserve parachute is a second parachute that a skydiver carries in case the main chute fails.

In the old days, reserve parachutes were worn in small packs in front of a jumper's stomach. Now they are worn most often in the back, near the main chute.

Main chutes are usually packed, or put into a bag, by the skydiver. But reserve chutes are always rigged by experts called riggers. These experts have special training and work very carefully. Like the air bag in a car, a reserve chute is an emergency device that a diver hopes he or she never has to use!

Altimeter

One of the most important things to know when you're skydiving is when to pull the ripcord. If you know how high you are when you jump, you can count or check a watch. If you do the math, you'll know how far you have fallen.

But that can be confusing when the earth is rushing toward you. That's why most skydivers use special altimeters that tell them how high they are.

An altimeter measures air pressure. Air pressure changes depending on your altitude. That's how you know how high you are. Airplane pilots use similar devices while flying.

Skydivers wear altimeters on their wrists like watches. Some altimeters are attached to earphones and beep when the diver reaches a certain altitude. These are sometimes called "dirt alerts," because they warn the jumper that the dirt is coming fast!

Extreme Fact

For safety's sake, skyboards are equipped with a special release. It's something like the ripcord. If there's a problem, the surfer can easily and quickly get his or her feet out of the board.

Automatic Activation Device (AAD)

Think of an automatic activation device (AAD) as a robot ripcord puller. It pulls the cord when it senses that the parachutist can't. Usually this device uses altitude and speed to decide when to come to the rescue. Student skydivers are required to have AADs attached to their rigs.

Training

Having the proper equipment is very important to a skydiver. But the most essential safety device is a skydiver's own training. Students have to go through many basic jumps before they can move on to harder ones. Every jump is carefully planned and thought out on the ground. It's like mapping a cross-country trip before setting out.

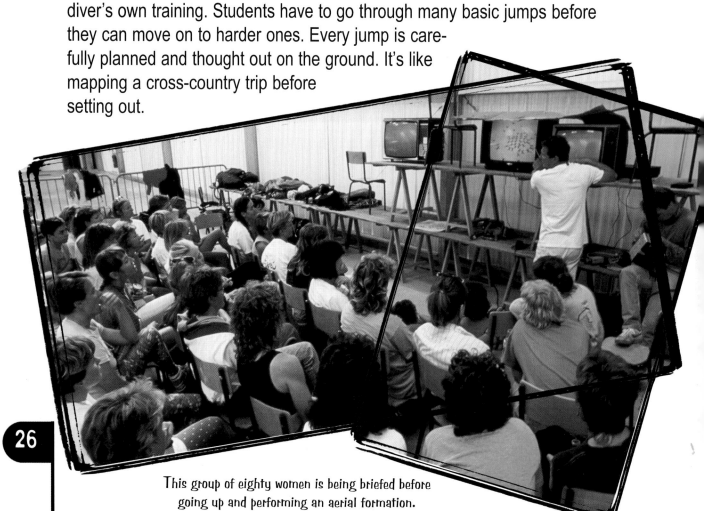

This group of eighty women is being briefed before going up and performing an aerial formation.

Basic Training

There's a lot more to skydiving than strapping on a parachute and jumping out of an airplane. Every diver has to learn some basic moves before he or she can try the really rad stuff.

The Arch

The first thing that every student learns is to arch. It's the basic element of a stable body position. The arch gives the skydiver a steady position in the air as he or she falls. It is also an easy position from which to pull the ripcord.

The arch is so basic that everyone learns it the first time he or she signs up for a jump. In fact, you can try it right now:

Stand with your legs relaxed and apart. Put your hands out flat and bend your arms at your elbows at a 90° angle. Your hands should be about even with your head. Pretend you're making an L with each arm. Or that someone has just shouted "Stick 'em up!" Now lift your shoulders and arch your back as if you're looking upward. Remember to keep the rest of your body in place.

the arch

That's it. Now that you can do it standing up, try it on your stomach. If you are arching properly, only your tummy will touch the ground.

If you bend your legs backward at the knees, you'll be in the box position, one of the most basic freefall positions. Spread your arms and legs out like Vs, and you'll be in a spread. Remember—arch, arch, arch!

Of course, everything feels just a little bit different when you're moving through the air at 100 feet per second.

When getting out of an airplane, a skydiver doesn't jump or push away. Instead he or she forms an arch and gently falls into the wind. The more relaxed the skydiver is, the easier the arch becomes. Once the wind takes over, the skydiver seems to float in the air. This is the freefall.

Freefall

Once in freefall there are many things a skydiver can do. Here are some of the basic moves:

Box

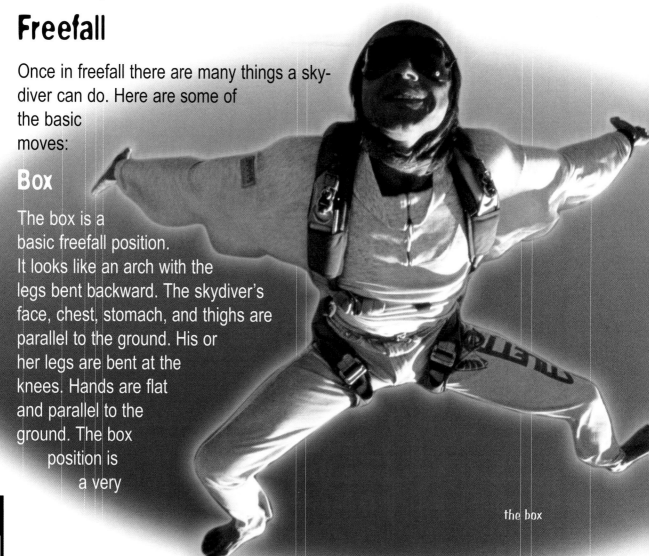

The box is a basic freefall position. It looks like an arch with the legs bent backward. The skydiver's face, chest, stomach, and thighs are parallel to the ground. His or her legs are bent at the knees. Hands are flat and parallel to the ground. The box position is a very

the box

natural one. The pros say that if the diver can relax during freefall, he or she will naturally end up in this position.

Some people call the box without an arch a "frog." That's because skydivers doing the box look like frogs leaping across a pond.

the delta

The Delta

The delta looks like a dive through the air. In this position the skydiver points his or her head and upper body toward the ground. The arms slant backward like the wings on a jet plane. The legs are straight and in a V. The delta position makes a skydiver go faster than the box does.

Parachuting Pioneer

Georgia Thompson ("Tiny") Broadwick was one of the first American women skydivers. In 1914 she made a jump that is often called the first freefall. Her father, Charles Broadwick, made parachutes.

29

The Track

If the delta isn't fast enough for you, you can always get on track. In this position, the diver slightly bends his or her head and body. The skydiver's body acts like a miniature airplane wing. The track can be very important when joining formations or getting into the right position.

Turns

Turns are actually pretty easy. The trick is being able to control them. The skydiver can make small turns by tilting the palms of his or her hands. Basic turns are made by tucking one shoulder down and twirling the body like a piece of licorice.

the barrel roll

Barrel Roll

In the barrel roll, a skydiver makes his or her body flip over like a rolling barrel. The basic move starts as a cross position, in which the arms are spread straight out like a cross. One arm is brought into the chest quickly. The body shoots downward and over. The diver pushes the arm back out and pulls in the other. Then he or she goes spread-eagle again as the dive is completed.

Loops

In a front loop, a skydiver tucks his or her head down and throws the feet backward, looping in the air. In the back loop, the opposite happens: The skydiver pushes his or her feet up and over the head, called a "full-gainer."

Skysurfing

Everything a water surfer can do, a skysurfer can do and then some. Using the wind as a never-ending wave, a skysurfer can twist, flip, or even helicopter the skyboard.

Skysurfing is a very tricky type of skydiving. Only experienced skydivers try it. Just as in all skydiving, body position is extremely important. Changing the position of an arm or leg changes the wind resistance. This makes a skydiver move in a certain way. In skysurfing, the surfer also moves the board. He or she must remember that the board meets the air differently than his or her arms and legs do.

Various lengths and widths of the board make a very big difference in the air.

One of the coolest skysurfing

Freefall Facts

 The fastest freefall ever recorded was 702 miles per hour. It was performed in 1960 by Captain Joseph W. Kittinger Jr., who stepped out of a balloon at 18,000 feet. His trip down took four and a half minutes.

 Standing during a freefall increases drop speed.

 No matter what you see on television, it's pretty much impossible to hold a conversation while in freefall because of the howling wind all around you.

moves is the helicopter. The skydiver pushes the board up overhead and spins upside down. From the side, the skyboard looks like the seed of a maple tree—what many people call a "helicopter"—as the surfer spins toward the ground.

Pulling the Ripcord

Obviously no one can freefall forever. After a few minutes of freefall, skydivers must pull the ripcord to slow their descent.

Pulling the ripcord is usually taught as part of a sequence, or a set of basic movements. Since timing is important, newbies are taught to repeat each step to themselves as they go through the sequence. Between steps most students learn to say "thousand," which helps them to count out the timing correctly. If you've ever been "it" in hide-and-seek, you already know how to do it.

Here's a basic sequence that newbies, or rookie skydivers, first learn:

"Arch thousand.": Arch. The most basic position has your hands about a foot from your
ears.

"Look thousand.": Still arching, look
down at the ripcord. Since you are still
arching, you may have to stretch your neck
down to the side a bit.

"Reach thousand.": Still arching, you reach
your right hand down and over to the ripcord. At
the same time, move your left hand above your head. The
left hand should be open and facing the ground—almost as
if you were signaling the ground to stop coming at you.

"Pull thousand.": Pull the ripcord!

"Arch thousand.": Put your hands and head back where
you started.

"Thousand one, thousand two, thousand three, thousand four, thousand five.": By the end of this count-
down, you should feel the opening shock. That's the sud-
den jerk of the parachute as it opens and you slow
down.

"Check thousand.": Look above you. Did the parachute
open? Are the lines clear? If so, enjoy the ride!

Steering the Chute

Once the parachute inflates, the skydiver can perform a whole new bunch of moves. He or she can steer to a landing zone. The skydiver can also fly the chute near others for more aerial tricks, or tricks in the air.

Modern parachutes are much easier to steer than the old round styles. Pulling the lines attached to the skydiver's harness changes the shape of the canopy, allowing it to be steered.

The harness's control handles are called steering toggles. They look a little bit like thin, plastic suitcase handles. They are located near the skydiver's head when the chute inflates, or fills with air. When a skydiver pulls down on the right toggle, it pulls down the back of the right corner of the parachute. That makes both the chute and the skydiver turn right. It also increases the speed.

Pulling both the right and left toggles at the same time slows the speed. This is called a flare. Modern parachutes can go as slow as five miles per hour. That's about the average speed of a kid walking to school, so you know it's nearly a crawl!

Landing

When landing, many skydivers go through different legs, or stages. These legs are similar to the steps a small airplane takes when landing. First the parachutist flies with the wind. Then he or she cuts across it. Finally the skydiver lands against the wind. The wind slows the parachute down, which makes for a very slow and soft landing.

Most newbies practice a parachute landing fall, or PLF, when they first start jumping. This is a safe way of falling when you are moving fast. You put your legs

Extreme Fact

No-wind land-
ings are harder
than those in a
gentle breeze.
That's because
the wind helps
slow you
down.

together and tuck your head forward. Then you let
your body turn as gently as possible, cushioning the
impact of falling on your side with a roll. It is almost
like turning your body into a shock absorber.

Skydiving Sensations

Oliver Furrer won the
bronze medal in the 1998 X
Games because of his unique
freestyle approach. Knut Krecker worked
the camera and dived with Furrer. Their
routine was very unusual because the
cameraman also did maneuvers instead of
just freefalling nearby.

Every skydive starts and ends the same way: up high and down low. It's what happens in between that makes things different— and interesting.

freestyle skydivers

Classical Skydiving

The most popular skydiving competitions are for accuracy and style. These are called classic or classical events because they are the oldest type of competition. They also test the most basic skills. Nearly every skydiver can

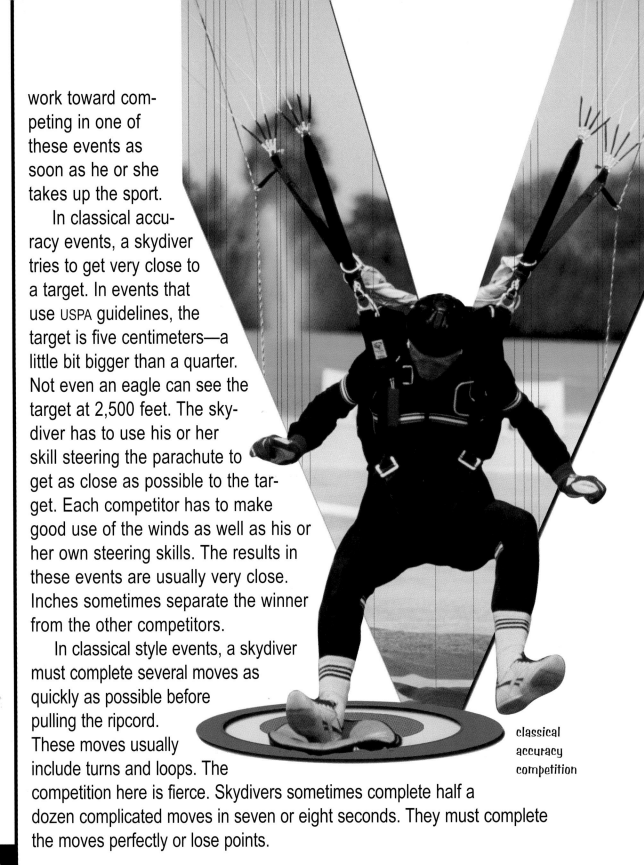

work toward competing in one of these events as soon as he or she takes up the sport.

In classical accuracy events, a skydiver tries to get very close to a target. In events that use USPA guidelines, the target is five centimeters—a little bit bigger than a quarter. Not even an eagle can see the target at 2,500 feet. The skydiver has to use his or her skill steering the parachute to get as close as possible to the target. Each competitor has to make good use of the winds as well as his or her own steering skills. The results in these events are usually very close. Inches sometimes separate the winner from the other competitors.

In classical style events, a skydiver must complete several moves as quickly as possible before pulling the ripcord. These moves usually include turns and loops. The

classical accuracy competition

competition here is fierce. Skydivers sometimes complete half a dozen complicated moves in seven or eight seconds. They must complete the moves perfectly or lose points.

Formation Skydiving

Relative work is what skydivers call it when they hang out together in midair. Teams jump from a plane, then "fly" themselves into a special design. Another name for this type of skydiving is freefall maneuvers. That name is appropriate, because the skydivers make their bodies into miniature airplanes as they maneuver or fly toward each other. They almost seem to be swimming in the air.

The official name for this skydiving style is freefall formation skydiving. This is because the skydivers link up, or dock, and make a formation or design in the sky. Some formations are called stars because that's what they look like from below. Since the divers are falling the entire time, there is a limited chance to link up. Only after separating do they open their chutes.

This large group of divers has completed docking for their formation.

Just connecting with each other can be tough, but some events require the skydivers to perform additional maneuvers once they join up. In some events these maneuvers are selected at random right before the jump. This makes practice very difficult. That's why a relative worker has to be more than just relatively good. He or she has to be an all-around great performer, able to work well with the team.

Canopy Formation

Skydivers don't just hang out together before pulling the ripcord. When they compete in canopy formation events, they come together once their parachutes are open. The open parachutes, or canopies, are like miniature airplane wings.

Teams of four or more skydivers make formations or race for the best time. This type of skydiving is also known as canopy relative work, or CRW. Usually skydivers refer to it with a word based on its abbreviation: "crew."

a thirteen-canopy formation

BASE

BASE is an acronym. It's a word made of the first letters of other words. BASE stands for "buildings, antennae, spans, and earth." BASE jumps are made from earth-bound objects like cliffs, buildings, and bridges. These jumps are quick—and scary. BASE jumpers need special equipment, and they must be very experienced sky-divers before trying this type of jump.

Only a few places allow BASE jumping. In the United States, one of the biggest annual BASE meets is Bridge Day in West Virginia. The jump is held at New River Gorge Bridge, 876 feet above ground. Jumpers usually deploy their chutes two or three seconds after leaving the bridge. A lot of jumpers end up in the river.

A skydiver BASE jumping from a bridge

41

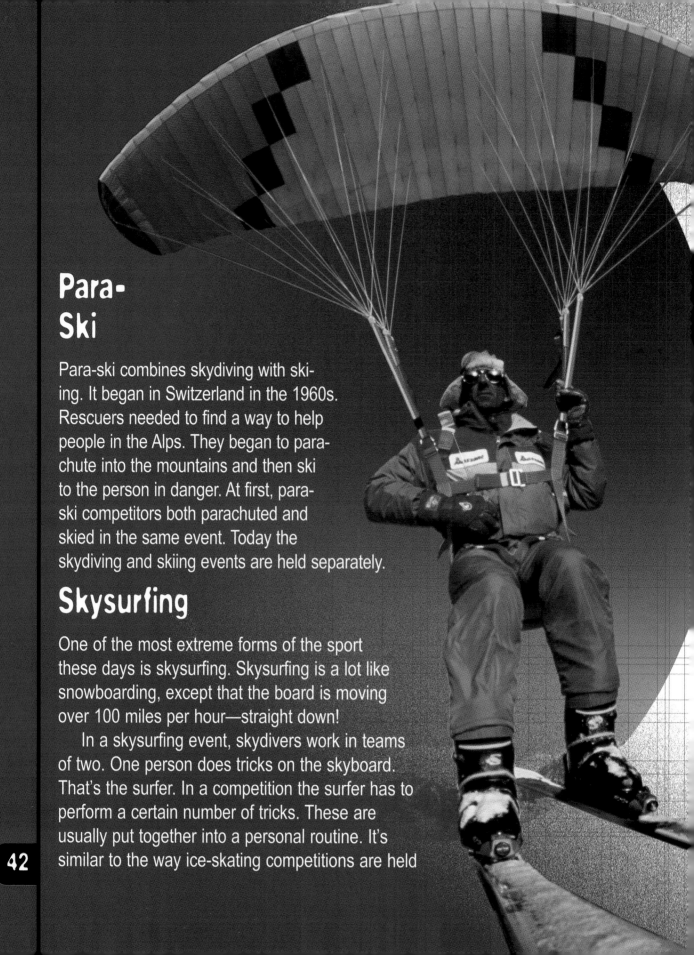

Para- Ski

Para-ski combines skydiving with skiing. It began in Switzerland in the 1960s. Rescuers needed to find a way to help people in the Alps. They began to parachute into the mountains and then ski to the person in danger. At first, para-ski competitors both parachuted and skied in the same event. Today the skydiving and skiing events are held separately.

Skysurfing

One of the most extreme forms of the sport these days is skysurfing. Skysurfing is a lot like snowboarding, except that the board is moving over 100 miles per hour—straight down!

In a skysurfing event, skydivers work in teams of two. One person does tricks on the skyboard. That's the surfer. In a competition the surfer has to perform a certain number of tricks. These are usually put together into a personal routine. It's similar to the way ice-skating competitions are held

in the Olympics. Judges look at style as well as technical skill.

The other member of the sky-surfing team is the cameraperson. This skydiver brings a special camera on the jump, which is usually attached to his or her helmet. The camera-person has to capture everything on video or film. The surfer gets all the glory, but the cameraperson's job is also very difficult. He or she must not only be able to "fly" close to the surfer but also get good pictures. If you've ever tried taking pictures of friends in a sporting event, you know how tough that can be. Imagine doing it several thousand feet above the earth, falling at over 100 miles per hour!

Both members of the team are judged in skysurfing competitions. The surfer's scores usually make up 75 per-cent of the total. The cameraperson's scores make up the rest. A great skysurfer needs a great cameraperson—and vice versa.

Freeflying

Freeflying is an advanced form of skydiving that is sometimes included in pro competitions. The athlete performs difficult maneuvers such as sitting during freefall. The maneuvers are choreographed into a routine which one or more skydivers can perform. Usually a cameraperson comes along to record the action.

Freeflying is also called freestyle and sitflying. That's because freeflying skydivers actually sit down on the job—at 10,000 feet.

Getting started in skydiving is easy. Grab the Yellow Pages and look under Parachute Jumping Instruction. A five-minute phone call is all it takes to get things rolling.

There are sky-diving centers and clubs nearly every-where. They are often called a drop zone, or "DZ," because, well, that's what's happening there, right? Skydivers are being dropped from above.

Usually DZs are located at smaller airports away from cities. Most if not all offer instruction for beginners as well as for advanced jumpers. Many feature special jumps and programs. Most will even hook you up with a videographer to capture your first jump for all time.

Some things to keep in mind before you sign on to jump:

Tandem Jumps

First-time divers looking for a no-fear, quick intro to the sport can try tandem jumps. In a tandem, the student is tied to a professional instructor. The instructor actually does all of the work—except the sweating.

Another great thing about tandem jumping is that you experience a real freefall the first time you jump. For at least forty seconds, you, along with your instructor, fly through the air with the greatest of ease.

Tandem jumping is meant as an introduction to the sport. To get serious a student must sign up for training programs.

tandem jump

Accelerated Freefall

A popular form of freefall training is called accelerated freefall, or AFF. A lot of skydivers say that this type of course gets you into the meat of the sport quicker than anything else. The first-time skydiver begins with a ground course that lasts about five or six hours. The student then makes his or her first jump with two instructors alongside. It's like parachuting with a pair of guardian angels. The instructors hold on to the student for a flight that lasts about fifty seconds. The student then pulls the ripcord and makes a solo canopy descent. That means that he or she gets to steer and land his or her own parachute. Really cool.

Static Line

Another type of training with a solo canopy descent is static line. In static line, the ripcord is pulled automatically. The student also takes a great first-jump course on the ground, which teaches him or her the basics. The

 Many programs have rules about age and weight.

 Usually you must be at least 18 years old to jump. However, some programs allow 16-year-olds to jump with a parent's permission. There has also been talk of lowering the age limit.

 You may need to make special arrangements if you're over a certain weight or not in good physical shape.

 Skydiving can be an expensive sport. First jumps usually cost more than $100. If you're serious about jumping, you'll have to buy special equipment. That can cost $1,000 or more. The cost of jumping becomes a lot less after the first time, however.

This group of divers is performing a static-line jump.

first-time jumper in a static program doesn't have a real freefall. Still, it's a totally awesome way to experience the sport.

USPA

Every skydiving class is a little different. Local instructors like to do what they have found works best. But there's always a lot of concern for safety. And the overall goal will always be the same: amazing experiences and safe landings.

If you're jumping in the United States, you'll want a program run by USPA members. You should also make sure that the drop zone is part of the USPA.

"Whuffer" is slang for someone who doesn't jump. It can be spelled in different ways, like "wuffo" and even "whutfo." It comes from the expression "What for you want to jump from an airplane, you crazy person, you?!"

The USPA sets national training guidelines. Pretty much everyone in U.S. skydiving is a member of this organization, but asking about it will show that you've done some homework. Usually schools supply equipment as well as instructors.

You don't have to be in Olympic shape to jump, but if you're wearing a full body cast, you may have a little trouble with some of the positions.

Seriously though, skydiving competitors are devoted athletes in top mental and physical condition. But first jumps are usually not too tough. Among the pros, injuries are nowhere near as common as newbies might think. Some enthusiasts say that skydiving is statistically the safest aviation sport.

The USPA has different ratings and licenses for skydivers. "Students" are total beginners. They always dive with an instructor. "Novices" have graduated from training but don't have a license yet.

The more you jump, the higher your license. A skydiver can get an A license after 20 freefalls. B comes after 50, C after 100, and D after 200. At each stage the parachutist must strut better and better stuff.

Extreme Fact
First jumps in an AFF program are usually made at least 9,000 feet above the ground. Chutes are deployed by 4,000 feet.

finally ready, equipment triple-checked, you clamber on board the plane psyched for your first jump. You're not nervous—at least not until the aircraft lurches skyward. That's when your stomach does its first belly flop.

Good thing you buckled your seatbelt.

You remind yourself that you don't have to jump, but there's no way you're going to wimp out now.

Your jumpmasters give you the thumbs-up. Time to prepare. The seatbelts are off; you're almost ready to jump. The pilot turns the airplane into the wind. This allows the aircraft to go "only" 100 miles per hour. That's the usual jump speed. Up front in the cockpit, the pilot is studying his instruments. Any second now, a cue from the global positioning satellite gear will tell him that he has found the drop zone.

The green light over the jump door snaps on. That's the signal everyone's been waiting for. The more experienced divers disappear into the empty blueness.

"Are you ready to SKYDIVE?" shouts your instructor.

"You bet," you say bravely, stepping toward the door. Your brain hits overload as you try to remember everything the instructor told you back on the ground. It seems like a million years—and just as many miles—since then.

Until you remember her favorite phrase:

"It's a Zen thing. Just take a breath, relax,
and do it."

You step to the door. The instructor and her
assistant stand on either side. They are both trained
jumpmasters. They've done this a million times.

But you haven't. Suddenly you're outside the
plane, standing on what has to be the tiniest step in
the world. And holding on for dear life. Somehow you
remember to look toward the front of the plane, then
the wing. You arch your body.

Are you really going to do this?

Your hands let go.

Both jumpmasters are right there with you, flying.

Flying!

8 Going for the Gold

Accomplished skydivers are serious athletes. Even an average jump is more exciting than ten basketball games put together. You can participate in the sport of skydiving whether or not you enter competitions.

However, competitions are a lot of fun. They help skydivers sharpen their skills. And for fans, they can be a great introduction to the sport.

Local clubs hold their

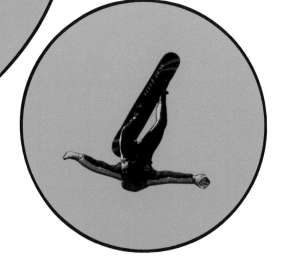

a skysurfing team competing in the X Games

own meets at various locations around the United States and the rest of the world. Competitors sometimes call these boogies or fun meets.

Traveling groups have skydiving competitions and exhibitions. Most of these events are sponsored by private groups and companies. The National Collegiate Parachuting Committee, the USPA, and many parachuting groups in other countries hold larger meets. All competitions usually include the classic events. Other forms of skydiving, like skysurfing, are also popular.

a team of skydivers hold hands during freefall

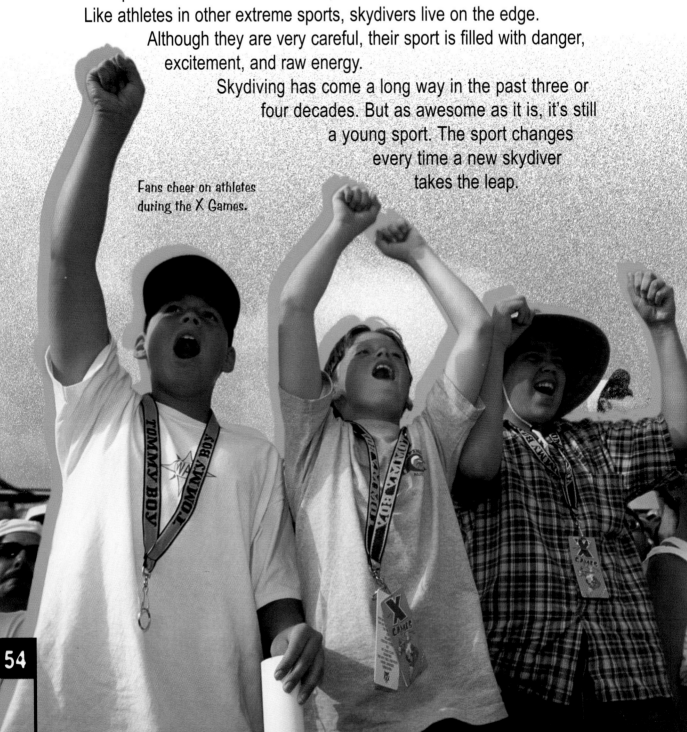

The highest level of competition in the United States is the National Parachuting Championships. The National Parachuting Championships are held every year. The big world meet is the World Parachuting Championships, which are held every other year. Also, skysurfing has now become part of the Summer X Games, which are broadcast on ESPN.

Like athletes in other extreme sports, skydivers live on the edge. Although they are very careful, their sport is filled with danger, excitement, and raw energy.

Skydiving has come a long way in the past three or four decades. But as awesome as it is, it's still a young sport. The sport changes every time a new skydiver takes the leap.

Fans cheer on athletes during the X Games.

"Skygod" is usually meant as an insult. A skygod—or a skygoddess—is someone who thinks he's an expert but just has a big ego. For example: "He thinks he's an awesome skygod, but he's really just a newbie."

What shape will the ultimate skyboard take? Will tomorrow's parachute be a triangle instead of a square? Can the pull of the earth be overcome for more than a few minutes?

We won't know until tomorrow. That's what makes this sport so extreme.

X-Planations

BASE A skydive from a building, an antenna, a span (such as a bridge), or the earth (such as a cliff). Special equipment is needed.

boogie A gathering of skydivers. Can be for competition or just for fun.

cell Part of a square canopy parachute. Most popular sport chutes have seven or nine of them.

CRW (pronounced "crew") This abbreviation stands for "canopy relative work." Skydivers open their parachutes and then fly in very close formation.

deploy To open the parachute.

dirt dive A ground practice of a skydive.

docking When two or more skydivers meet in the air to make a formation.

drop zone The skydiving center. Also called a DZ.

flare Pulling down on both steering toggles at the same time. This is used in landings to make the parachute slow down.

floaters Skydivers on the outside of the plane who are preparing to jump.

freestyle A type of skydiving in which the diver does different maneuvers; also called freeflying.

grippers Places for other skydivers to grab on to a jumpsuit during formation flying.

rig The entire parachute, including the main and reserve canopies.

rigger An expert who packs the reserve parachute. He or she also packs students' main parachutes.

square A ram-air parachute. Called a square to show that it's different from the old types of parachutes, which were round.

tandem A jump in which two skydivers are attached to one parachute.

Skydiving Organizations

Canadian Sport Parachuting Organization (CSPA)
4185 Dunning Road
Navan, ON K4B 1J1
(613) 835-3731
Web site: http://www.cspa.ca/
e-mail: office@cspa.ca

Christian Skydivers Association
P.O. Box 1451
Valrico, FL 33595-1451
(813) 737-1235

Fédération Aéronautique Internationale (FAI)
Avenue Mon Repos 24, CH-1005
Lausanne, Switzerland
41-21-345-1070
Web site: http://airsports.fai.org

National Aeronautics Association
1815 North Fort Myer Drive, Suite 700
Arlington, VA 22209
(703) 527-0226

The National Skydiving League
1728 Pine Street
DeLand, FL 32724
(904) 734-1598

United States Parachute Association (USPA)
1440 Duke Street
Alexandria, VA 22314
(703) 836-3495
Web site: http://www.uspa.org
e-mail: uspa@uspa.org

Web Sites

http://espn.go.com/extreme/index.html
http://www.aero.com/publications/parachutes/parachut.htm
http://www.afn.org/skydive
http://www.bpa.org.uk
http://www.dropzone.com
http://www.dropzone.com/skydive/ring/ring.shtml
http://www.enclave.com
http://www.flyboyz.com
http://www.gravityseekers.com
http://www.pcap.com/flyaway.htm
http://www.skydive.net
http://www.skydiveu.com
http://www.skyleague.com
http://www.skyzine.com
http://www.ssiprotour.com
http://www.ycg.org

Skydiving is taught and practiced at "drop zones" (DZs) or skydiving centers all across the country. The easiest way to find one is to look in the Yellow Pages under Parachute Jumping Instruction or Skydiving Instruction. You can also find DZs through listings with the United States Parachute Association and other groups—see our organization list or use the Web.

As if falling out of the sky isn't enough fun, some skydivers have begun jumping indoors. Well, kind of. Actually, they use a training device called a vertical wind tunnel. Skydivers "fly" on a column of air as they practice their maneuvers. Developed by the military, the skydiving simulations are just starting to be used by the public. Two of the first in the United States are operated by Flyaway—one in Las Vegas, Nevada, and the other in Pigeon Forge, Tennessee. Along with classes and training sessions, both centers allow visitors—if you contact them first.

Just like to watch? That's cool. Skydiving is part of the X Games on television. Want to check it out in the flesh rather than soaking in video rays? *No problemo*. Many DZs hold "boogies," or friendly skydiving competitions, most of which are open to spectators. Wild skysurfing and freeflying meets are sponsored by various organizations. You can find a list of meets on the Sky Sportif International Web site (http://www.ssiprotour.com). SSI is dedicated to staying on top of the sport. It's not just their hobby; it's their job.

Parachute demonstrations have become a popular part of many air shows, county fairs, and other activities. Local tourist groups often advertise them months in advance. You can find out about them through local newspapers or by contacting regional tourist groups. If your county or region has a Web page, you may find upcoming events listed there.

Extreme Reading

Books

George, Linda, and Charles George. *Team Skydiving*. Danbury, CT: Franklin Watts, 1998.

Lund, Bill, and Pat Ryan. *Sky Surfing*. Mankato, MN: Capstone Press, 1998.

Meeks, Christopher. *Skydiving*. Mankato, MN: Capstone Press, 1994.

Paulsen, Gary. *Skydive!* New York: Yearling, 1996.

Challenging Reading

Poynter, Dan, and Mike Turoff. *Parachuting: The Skydiver's Handbook*. Santa Barbara, CA: Para Publishing, 1998.

United States Parachute Association. *The Skydiver's Information Manual*. Alexandria, VA: USPA, 1998.

Magazines

Parachutist Magazine
The United States Parachute Association publishes *Parachutist Magazine* free for all members.
1440 Duke Street
Alexandria, VA 22314
(703) 836-3495

Skydiving
$16 per year.
1725 North Lexington Avenue
DeLand, FL 32724
(904) 736-4793

Index

Credits

About the Author

Jeremy Roberts is the pen name of Jim DeFelice. Jim often uses this name when he writes for young readers, which he tries to do as much as he can. Besides extreme sports books on sky-diving and climbing for Rosen Publishing, Jim's recent nonfiction includes biographies on King Arthur and Joan of Arc. He has written several installments in the *Eerie, Indiana*, series and a bunch of horror stories. His books for adults include techno-thrillers and a historical trilogy. Jim lives with his wife and son in a haunted farmhouse in upstate New York. His latest hobby is learning to fly airplanes, not jumping from them—but for some reason his flight instructor still calls him "The Rock."

Photo Credits

Series Design

Oliver Halsman Rosenberg

Layout

Laura Murawski

Consulting Editor

Amy Haugesag